Me:
Without Reservation

A Young Woman's Guide
to Bravery and Resilience

SO BRAVE

SO BRAVE

So Brave is committed as Australia's Young Women's Breast Cancer Charity to raise awareness for all young women across Australia to be #breastaware.

Our mission is clear: we empower young women diagnosed with breast cancer; raise awareness and educate young women to be #breastaware and fundraise for breast cancer research.

EMPOWERMENT Our So Brave Model Ambassador program works with young breast cancer survivors to raise awareness that young women get breast cancer too and to fund research to change the future for the next generation. These fabulous and brave young women who are candidates for this annual program would love your support, so that they might participate in their own amazing paint days just like the women you see in the pages of our past Calendars. If you are interested in learning more about becoming an Ambassador, our support programs for young breast cancer survivors or in supporting our candidates, please get in touch and get involved.

EDUCATION So Brave, in collaboration with high schools and universities, delivers a high impact, engaging and relevant program of positive body image and empowering young women to become their own best health advocates.
If you want So Brave to come to your school or university, please get in touch!

RESEARCH Working with young women across Australia, So Brave will be undertaking a body of work to investigate the real impact of breast cancer on young women in Australia. If you would like to participate in this study, we would very much like to talk to you!

YOUNG WOMEN Under the So Brave banner, So Brave's Young Women's Advisory Committee, BraveYou allows young women (15-25) to take leadership and community advocacy roles, in the breast awareness space but also on a wide range of health topics in addition to breast health and awareness. If you're interested in getting involved, please contact us at sobrave.com.au/braveyou

ISBN 978-0-6487992-2-1

© 2020 So Brave Ltd.

Please keep following our journey:

 /SOBRAVEPROJECT

#SOBRAVE   #SOBRAVEPROJECT   #BREASTAWARE   #FEELITONTHEFIFTH
#YOUNGBREASTCANCER   #BREASTCANCEREDUCATION

SOBRAVE.COM.AU

Disclaimer

So Brave Ltd does not purport to give specific health advice nor is any information contained herein a substitute for health or medical advice from a qualified professional. The opinions expressed in this publication are those of the authors. They do not purport to reflect the opinions or views of So Brave Ltd and So Brave Ltd expressly disclaims all liability of any kind.

Foreword

So Brave, as the only breast cancer charity in Australia specifically advocating for and representing young women, has worked with hundreds of young women over the past 5 years:

Empowering

our So Brave Model Ambassadors, who are all young breast cancer survivors to face their fears and embrace their bodies;

Educating

high-school students, university students and volunteers to become #breastaware and strong advocates for themselves, and for their community to initiate change;

Guiding

our interns and the young women we work with through not only some of their first experiences in the workforce, but also educating them to be #breastaware, how to apply their skills and knowledge to their lives and how to find their strength to bring about change; and

Leading

the industry in recognising the specific needs of young women facing and experiencing breast cancer, bringing change within the breast cancer charity-sector, medical profession and broader community.

We have watched those young women embrace themselves, exude newfound confidence, expand their knowledge, and come closer to discovering their incredible potential.

We have teamed up with some incredible experts across a number of diverse fields to share their invaluable knowledge with you to cover off on absolutely everything to help you become...

Me: Without Reservation

Courage

IS BEING

yourself

EVERYDAY

IN A WORLD THAT

tells you to be

SOMEONE ELSE

Contents

FOREWORD	3
SO FOCUSED: GOALS AND VISION	7
SO AWARE: BREAST AWARE	19
SO LOVED: RELATIONSHIPS	35
SO CHERISHED: SELF-CARE	45
SO MINDFUL: MENTAL HEALTH	59
SO COURAGEOUS: SELF-ADVOCACY	69
SO SAVVY: FINANCIAL FITNESS	83
SO CONFIDENT: SELF-ESTEEM AND CONFIDENCE	97
SO HEALTHY: HEALTH AND WELLNESS	107
SO POWERFUL: SEXUAL HEALTH	119
FINAL WRAP UP: TOWARDS BRAVERY AND RESILIENCE	131
THANK YOU	134
KEEP IN TOUCH	136

We cannot all succeed when half of us are held back. We call upon our sisters around the world to be brave – to embrace the strength within themselves and realize their full potential.

MALALA YOUSAFZAI

So Focused
Goals and Vision

There is no limit to what we,
as women, can accomplish.

MICHELLE OBAMA

In her footsteps

SARA BLAKELY

Sara's journey began at the dinner table of her childhood home. Her father would ask her and her brothers what had been their biggest failures that week. Not only would her dad encourage them to share their failures, but he would celebrate them.

> "MY DAD WOULD ENCOURAGE ME ANY TIME SOMETHING DIDN'T GO THE WAY I EXPECTED IT TO, OR MAYBE I GOT EMBARRASSED BY A SITUATION, TO WRITE DOWN WHERE THE HIDDEN GIFTS WERE AND WHAT I GOT OUT OF IT."

This ultimately redefined failure for her. So, when she wanted to be a lawyer but failed the LSAT, only to get offered a chipmunk position at Disneyland when she tried out for Goofy, she kept going. This led her to accept an offer to sell fax machines door-to-door for seven years. It was there at age 41 where she discovered a gap in the market and sparked an idea that became a global sensation. Committed to her idea, with little to no industry knowledge and no reason not to try, Sara Blakely became the founder of Spanx. She is now recognised as one of the most successful self-made women in the world. When asked the secret to her success: she attests it to failure.

> Failure for me became not trying, versus the outcome.
>
> **SARA BLAKELY**

CAN YOU THINK OF YOUR BIGGEST "OOPSIES", AS SARA CALLS THEM? WRITE DOWN WHAT MAKES YOU GRATEFUL FOR EXPERIENCING THEM?

....
....
....
....
....
....
....
....

HOW DOES THIS CHANGE YOUR VIEW OF FAILURE?

....
....
....
....
....
....
....
....

WHEN THINKING ABOUT YOUR GOALS IN LIFE - CAREER, HEALTH, FAMILY, RELATIONSHIPS, PERSONAL - WHAT IS IMPORTANT TO YOU?

....
....
....
....

WHY IS IT IMPORTANT TO YOU?

....
....
....
....

FINISH THIS SENTENCE: IF I WEREN'T AFRAID I WOULD…

....
....
....
....

WHAT ARE SOME GOALS YOU CURRENTLY HAVE?

....
....
....
....

HOW ARE YOU WORKING TOWARDS THESE GOALS?

....
....
....
....

The greatest glory in living,
lies not in never falling,
but in rising
every time we fall

UNKNOWN

The 10 x 10 challenge

Sometimes it's hard to know what goals to go for. This quick little exercise will help to unlock your curiosity!

Every day for the next 10 days, write down two lists - 10 things that you love to do, and 10 things that you're really good at.

Love to do	Really good at

P.S. You already know what it is your heart desires!

> Find out who you are, and do it on purpose
>
> **DOLLY PARTON**

In her footsteps

MELANIE PERKINS

Do you have a dream? How much do you believe in your dream? Let's say you pitch your dream to 10 people. Each one rejects you. Do you still believe in your dream? Then you pitch to another 10, then another until you have opened your heart to 100 people and no one believes in you. Do you find a new dream?

Melanie Perkins, far from her Perth home and living on her brother's floor, pitched to over 100 Silicon Valley venture capitalists each of whom rejected her idea. Melanie, the founder of *Canva*, is now the third richest woman in Australia.

When she was just 19, Melanie realised while teaching a basic computer design course just how difficult using current technology designing and printing could be. She left university with only her final semester left and focused on *Fusion Yearbooks*. After learning how to kite surf of all things, Melanie was able to impress Silicon Valley venture capitalist Bill Mai (a kite surfing expert) who later introduced her to some of her very first investors including celebrities Woody Harrelson and Owen Wilson.

More than 20 million people in 190 countries are using *Canva* which is now valued at $US 6 billion.

HAVE YOU FOUND YOUR PASSION IN LIFE YET?   YES / NO

HOW FAR WOULD YOU GO TO ACCOMPLISH YOUR DREAMS?

SO FOCUSED

LOOKING BACK AT YOUR 10 X 10 CHALLENGE, DID YOU DISCOVER SOME NEW THINGS ABOUT YOURSELF? HAS THIS INSPIRED SOME NEW DREAMS?

HOW ABOUT SETTING SOME MINI GOALS TO HELP YOU GET THERE?

Check in

HOW ARE YOU GOING WITH YOUR GOALS?

....
....
....
....

TAKE SOME TIME THIS WEEK AND ASK - WHAT DID I ACCOMPLISH? WHAT DIDN'T I DO? WHAT WILL I DO DIFFERENTLY NEXT WEEK?

....
....
....
....
....
....
....

WHAT FEELINGS CAME UP FOR YOU? WAS THIS TIME TO REFLECT USEFUL?

....
....
....
....

SO FOCUSED

HOW DID YOU FAIL THIS WEEK?

WHAT DID YOU LEARN FROM IT?

CONSIDER SETTING ASIDE 10 MINUTES EACH WEEK TO ASSESS WHAT YOU HAVE DONE AND WHAT YOU CAN DO NEXT WEEK

Believe in your dreams!

Step out of the history that is holding you back.

Step into the new story you are willing to create.

OPRAH WINFREY

So Aware
Breast Aware

One in seven Australian women — mothers, sisters, wives, daughters, friends — will be diagnosed with breast cancer in their lifetime.

In her footsteps

KYLIE MINOGUE

Kylie Minogue was diagnosed with breast cancer when she was just 36 years old. The Australian singer was initially misdiagnosed and was only able to start treatment weeks later after getting a second opinion. She encourages women to trust their instincts and says,

"BECAUSE SOMEONE IS IN A WHITE COAT AND USING BIG MEDICAL INSTRUMENTS DOESN'T NECESSARILY MEAN THEY'RE RIGHT."

HOW IMPORTANT IS CHECKING AND BECOMING FAMILIAR WITH YOUR BREASTS TO YOU AND WHY?

WHO IN YOUR LIFE DO YOU KNOW THAT'S HAD BREAST CANCER?

Share the love with someone who's experiencing breast cancer today with So Brave's book for young breast cancer survivors and their friends and family.

Letters of Love to our New Breast Friends – get your copies at **sobrave.com.au/love**

I AM TOUGH

I AM BRAVE

I AM STRONG

How to be #BREASTAWARE

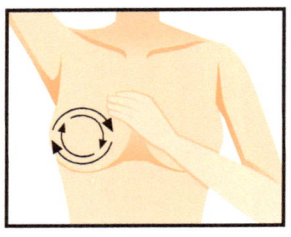

CHECK your breasts and the area around them regularly. Breast changes can include lumps, skin and nipple changes, pain and changes in breast size or shape.

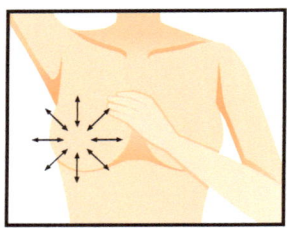

If you **DETECT** a change, book in with a GP as soon as possible to get a referral for imaging.

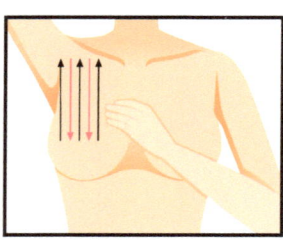

FOLLOW UP with your doctor, and return earlier if you notice further changes.

Find out about your **FAMILY HISTORY** of breast and ovarian cancer.

This information is a guide only and does not constitute comprehensive medical advice. Consult your doctor for more information and specific advice.

To download our complete *breast awareness guide* and get monthly breast check reminders, register now at **sobrave.com.au/breastaware**

Knowing your family cancer history is important and provide eligibility for additional screening in young women.

1 in 10 women will be affected by breast cancer due to an inherited gene defect.

Although breast cancer appears to run in families, a lack of family history doesn't remove the risk of developing breast cancer.

In her footsteps

BREEANNA

"I WAS DIAGNOSED WITH BREAST CANCER 7 DAYS BEFORE MY 22ND BIRTHDAY, AND HAD MY FIRST SESSION OF CHEMO 2 WEEKS LATER. I WAS DIAGNOSED WITH STAGE 4 METASTATIC HER2 POSITIVE BREAST CANCER - WHICH HAD SPREAD FROM MY BREAST TO MY LYMPH NODES AND I HAVE THREE LESIONS ON MY LIVER. I'VE FINISHED ALL MY CHEMO NOW, BUT WILL BE ON TREATMENT OF ANOTHER THERAPY CALLED HERCEPTIN AND PERJETA EVERY 3 WEEKS INDEFINITELY.

THANKFULLY, MY LAST SCANS ARE SHOWING THAT EVERYTHING HAS SHRUNK AND I HAVE NOW HAD A RIGHT-SIDE MASTECTOMY AND 21 LYMPH NODES IN MY ARMPIT REMOVED. THERE IS ALSO THE POSSIBILITY OF LIVER SURGERY IN THE FUTURE.

I WANT TO SHARE MY STORY, BECAUSE IT IS UPSETTING THAT THERE IS NOT MUCH OUT THERE FOR YOUNG WOMEN WHO ARE DIAGNOSED WITH BREAST CANCER. I'M DEALING WITH THE UPS AND DOWNS THAT COME WITH TREATMENT BUT I ALSO WANT TO EDUCATE PEOPLE THAT THIS CAN HAPPEN AT ANY AGE."

HOW DO YOU FEEL KNOWING THAT YOUNG WOMEN GET BREAST CANCER?

....
....
....

WHAT ARE SOME MYTHS/MISCONCEPTIONS YOU'VE HEARD ABOUT YOUNG WOMEN AND BREAST CANCER?

....
....
....
....

#feelitonthefifth

Put a reminder in your phone and don't forget to *feel it on the fifth* of every month!

Breast tissue can change during the month with a woman's hormonal cycle, so checking on roughly the same day of your cycle is the best way of monitoring your breasts.

In her footsteps

YVONNE

Yvonne was diagnosed with an aggressive form of breast cancer at 37 years old. She had no family history of breast cancer. First discovering the changes in her breasts at 36 she was told she was too young for a mammogram. Her voice went unheard and the changes were dismissed as a hormonal lump post breast feeding.

She has now undergone a single mastectomy, chemotherapy and drug therapy. As unbelievably hard as it has been for her, her husband and two young children, the biggest hit for Yvonne has been to her body image post mastectomy.

"ONE BREAST MISSING, NO HAIR, EXTRA KILOS, THE TEARS IN MY EYES. IT HAS TAKEN MORE FROM ME THAN I'M WILLING TO ADMIT AND MORE THAN PEOPLE ARE ABLE TO SEE. I WANT TO EMPOWER YOUNG WOMEN TO KNOW THEIR BODIES, UNDERSTAND CHANGES AND HELP THEM BE THEIR BEST ADVOCATE FOR THEMSELVES.

WOMEN NEED TO KNOW THEY HAVE A RIGHT TO REQUEST TESTS, TO SEEK A SECOND OR EVEN THIRD OPINION IF THAT IS WHAT IT TAKES. TO KNOW THAT THIS DISEASE DOES NOT DISCRIMINATE BASED ON AGE, YOUNG WOMEN GET BREAST CANCER TOO."

WHAT IS YOUR PLAN FOR BECOMING BREAST AWARE?

BREAST CANCER DOESN'T DISCRIMINATE

I HOPE YOU ARE
empowered

WITH THE
strength

I KNOW IS
inside you

WHEN DID YOU LAST DO A BREAST CHECK?

DO YOU KNOW YOUR NORMAL — WHAT IS THAT FOR YOU?

DO YOU KNOW YOUR FAMILY CANCER HISTORY? IF NOT, WHAT DO YOU NEED TO DO TO FIND OUT?

In her footsteps

BECK

> "I WAS 29, YOUNG, FIT AND HEALTHY. THERE WAS NO WAY I WAS EXPECTING TO BE TOLD THE WEEK OF CHRISTMAS 2017 THAT I HAD BREAST CANCER!"

Beck was diagnosed with a very aggressive type of cancer called Triple Negative Breast Cancer. There are limited treatment options and has a significantly lower 5 year survival rate than other forms of breast cancer. She had no family history and her genetic testing came back negative.

Beck now aims to make a difference by raising awareness about breast cancer and the importance of doing monthly checks. As an ambassador for So Brave she is part of the community that helps educate young women to be #breastaware and support young women affected by the disease.

> "YOU CAN'T ALWAYS CHANGE WHAT HAPPENS TO YOU, BUT YOU CAN CHANGE HOW YOU RESPOND TO IT."

LET'S START A CONVERSATION: WHO ARE YOU GOING TO SHARE THE BREAST AWARENESS MESSAGE WITH?

Do you need help in sharing this message? So Brave has many resources and can also provide online seminars — just get in touch!

/SOBRAVEPROJECT

SOBRAVE.COM.AU/BREASTAWARE

All women, regardless of age, should be aware of how their breasts look and feel.

#besmart. Be #breastaware.

Early detection and regular breast checks every month might just save your life.

Check in

DO YOU FEEL MORE CONFIDENT PERFORMING A BREAST CHECK?

....
....
....
....
....

WHAT WAS YOUR BIGGEST TAKEAWAY FROM THIS SECTION?

....
....
....
....
....
....
....
....

WHAT INFORMATION WILL YOU SHARE WITH YOUR FRIENDS AND FAMILY?

....
....
....
....

So Loved

Relationships

Surround yourself only with people who are going to take you higher.

OPRAH WINFREY

In her footsteps

KRISTEN BELL

How do you know if you are in a toxic relationship? Kristen Bell has described that her first year of marriage to her long-time husband Dax Shepard was indeed toxic. Her go-to in the middle of a fight would be to yell something, slam the door, get in her car and speed off around the corner. While it felt good, she only realised how toxic it was to their relationship when her husband pointed it out.

While they admit their marriage hasn't been easy, both Kristen and Dax have publicly shared how they have maintained the healthy relationship we see now for over a decade.

WHAT IS YOUR BIGGEST WEAKNESS IN RELATIONSHIPS?

....
....
....
....

HOW DO YOU THINK YOU COULD ACTIVELY WORK TO DO BETTER?

....
....
....
....

DESCRIBE THE TRAITS THAT ARE IMPORTANT TO YOU IN A HEALTHY RELATIONSHIP?

> I still have friends from primary school.
> And my two best girlfriends are from secondary school. I don't have to explain anything to them.
> I don't have to apologise for anything.
> They know. There's no judgment in any way.
>
> **EMMA WATSON**

HOW DO YOU EXPRESS YOUR EMOTIONS TO OTHERS?

....
....
....
....
....
....
....

DO YOU FEEL LIKE YOU ARE BEING HEARD AND APPRECIATED IN YOUR RELATIONSHIPS?

....
....
....
....
....
....
....

WHAT DOES A TOXIC RELATIONSHIP LOOK LIKE TO YOU?

....
....
....
....
....
....
....

Top *12 signs* it's time to **move on** from a **relationship**

1 When you **live in past memories** more than the present

2 When the relationship **brings you more pain** than joy

3 When he/she expects you to **change**

4 When you stay on, **expecting** he/she will **change**

5 When you keep **justifying** his/her **actions** to yourself

6 When he/she is causing you **emotional/physical/verbal hurt**

7 When the **same situation/issue recurs** even though you tried addressing it

8 When he/she **puts little to no effort** in the relationship

9 When your **fundamental values** and **beliefs** are **different**

10 When the relationship **holds you back**, hence **preventing** both of you from **growing as individuals**

11 When you stay on **expecting things to get better**

12 When neither of you **feel the same way** about each other

'How to move on from a relationship' by Celestine Chua - Personal Excellence - personalexcellence.co

In her footsteps

OPRAH AND GAYLE

Oprah Winfrey and Gayle King grew up in two different worlds. Oprah in poverty moving between houses and Gayle in Turkey with a housekeeper and a swimming pool. Yet, their friendship has lasted for over 40 years. The pair had their first encounter as young journalists working in different departments at the Baltimore's WJZ station. A snow storm hit one evening and even though the girls were just colleagues, Oprah offered Gayle to stay at her place nearby rather than try to get home. They talked all night and have remained best friends ever since.

Throughout the years they have been each other's shoulder to cry on, someone to listen to, share with and be their best cheerleader. Before Gayle became the star of CBS's *This Morning*, Oprah had become extremely successful with her own talk show.

Oprah often tells the story of when she found $482 in the pocket of her coat when Gayle was visiting her in Chicago. When she asked Gayle if she wanted it she told her to keep it. Years later Gayle told Oprah that when she arrived home that night she thought of all the things she could have done with that cash, like paid her electric bill and bought groceries. When Oprah asked Gayle why she didn't say something, she replied that she never wanted her to think that she was out to get something or take advantage.

So how did they make it all these years? Gayle never felt that she lived in Oprah's shadow, they were both always happy with their own lives. Showing us all that a true friend should never take advantage of you or be jealous of your success.

WHO IS THE GAYLE TO YOUR OPRAH?

WHEN LOOKING AT YOUR FRIENDSHIP CIRCLE, ARE YOU SURROUNDING YOURSELF WITH PEOPLE WHO ARE HAPPY IN THEIR OWN LIVES?

....
....

HOW DO THEY RESPOND WHEN SOMETHING POSITIVE HAPPENS IN YOUR LIFE?

....
....
....
....
....

HOW HAVE YOU BEEN UNKIND TO THOSE YOU LOVE?

....
....
....
....
....

HOW CAN YOU ADDRESS THIS?

....
....
....
....
....

In her footsteps

SMITH FAMILY

When Willow Smith was just nine years old, she brought her mother Jada Pinkett Smith to a great realisation: that she did not know her. She knew her as a mother, but not as a person.

Since then Jada has been on a journey to open up to her daughter about her own history and gradually work on their relationship. Now the Smith family share their intimate thoughts and stories to a global audience of almost 10 million followers on their Facebook watch series, *Red Table Talk*. The hosts are three generations of women: Jada Pinkett Smith (herself), her daughter, Willow and her mum, Adrienne Banfield-Norris. They have covered a range of topics including polyamorous relationships, racial divisions, addiction, sex, mental illness and more. The show not only gives insight to the three intergenerational perspectives on global issues but is a way to create conversations in their family to get to know each other better.

HOW MUCH DO YOU REALLY KNOW ABOUT YOUR OWN FAMILY?

For people to be able to sit down together and have a conversation, that's the power of love. Love is what sometimes holds us and binds us when we're not so happy.

JADA PINKETT-SMITH

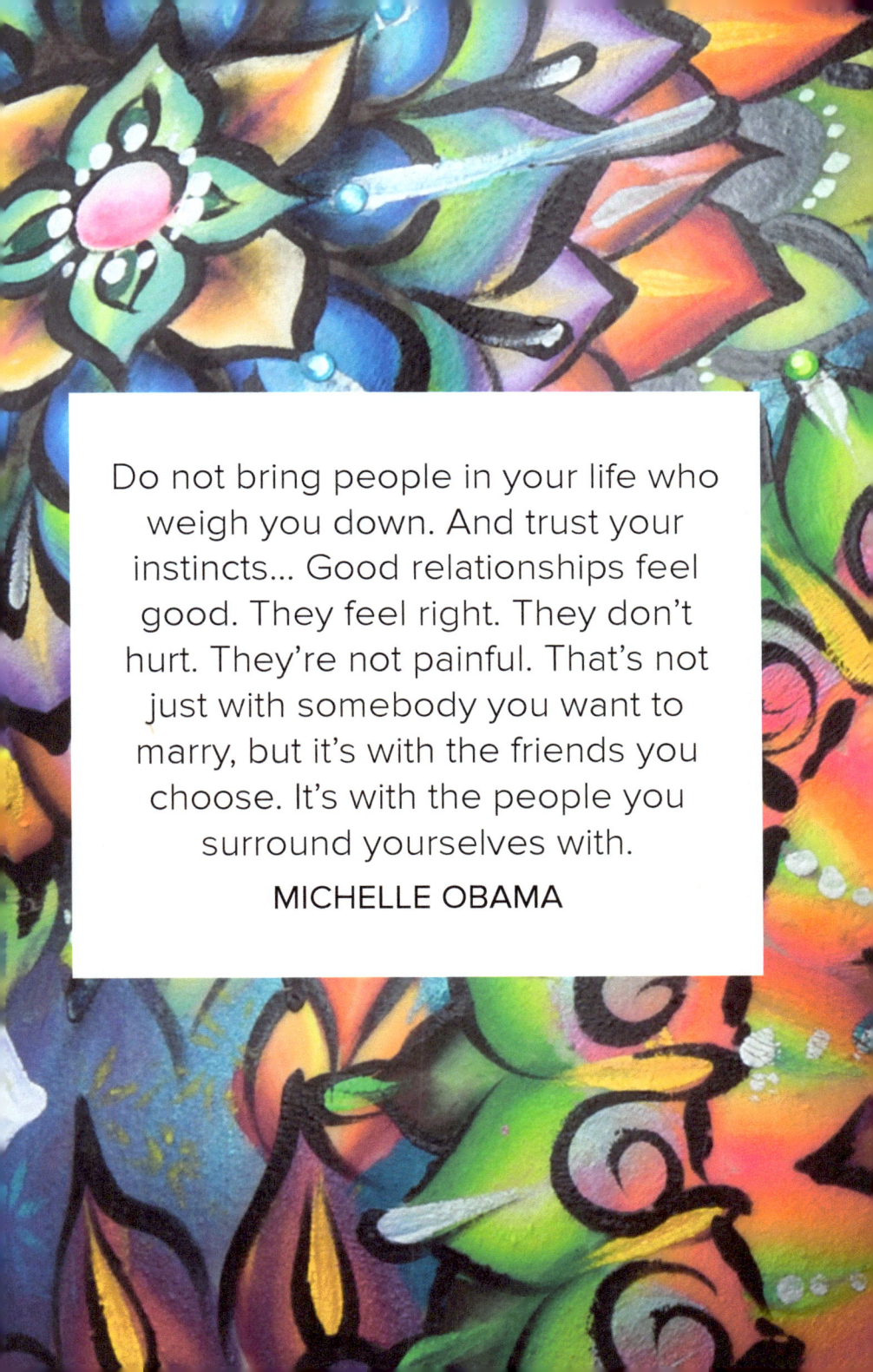

Do not bring people in your life who weigh you down. And trust your instincts... Good relationships feel good. They feel right. They don't hurt. They're not painful. That's not just with somebody you want to marry, but it's with the friends you choose. It's with the people you surround yourselves with.

MICHELLE OBAMA

Check in

WHO ARE YOU GRATEFUL TO HAVE IN YOUR LIFE? WHO MAKES YOU FEEL GOOD ABOUT YOURSELF?

FAMILY ....
....

FRIENDS ....
....

COLLEAGUES ....
....

ROMANTIC PARTNERS ....
....

WHO MAKES YOU FEEL GOOD ABOUT YOURSELF? MAKE A LIST OF ALL THE BEAUTIFUL PEOPLE WHO HAVE SUPPORTED YOU AND WHAT YOU LOVE MOST ABOUT THEM.

....
....
....
....
....
....
....
....

SEND THEM A MESSAGE TODAY TO REMIND THEM HOW MUCH YOU LOVE AND APPRECIATE THEM!

So Cherished
Self-care

We just need to be kinder to ourselves. If we treated ourselves the way we treated our best friend, can you imagine how much better off we would be?

MEGHAN MARKLE

In her footsteps

LIZ GILBERT

Elizabeth Gilbert, author of *Eat, Pray, Love* treats self-care, how you should treat an animal brought home from the shelter.

> "NOW IMAGINE THIS: IT'S YOUR FIRST NIGHT HOME ALONE WITH THAT DOG, AND SHE'S TREMBLING IN FEAR. HOW WOULD YOU TREAT HER? WOULD YOU SCREAM AT HER AND TELL HER SHE'S AN IDIOT? WOULD YOU KICK HER? WOULD YOU LOCK HER IN A DARK ROOM ALL ALONE? WOULD YOU STARVE HER OR LET HER BINGE-EAT A BUNCH OF GARBAGE? WOULD YOU LET HER STAY IN AN ENVIRONMENT WHERE OTHER DOGS ATTACK HER EVERY DAY?"

> "YOU WOULD OFFER HER A WARM AND SAFE BED, RIGHT? HEALTHY FOOD. A COSY ENVIRONMENT. WALKS IN THE SUNSHINE. FRESH AIR AND CLEAN WATER. CAREFUL SOCIALIZATION WITH OTHER ANIMALS — NICE ONES THAT DON'T BITE. NAPS. TENDERNESS. AFFECTION. PLAYTIME. AND LOTS OF PATIENCE. THAT'S HOW YOU LOVE AN ANIMAL."

HOW ARE YOU TREATING YOURSELF RIGHT NOW?

WHAT CAN YOU DO TO MAKE YOURSELF FEEL BETTER?

Have you ever written a letter to yourself?

You may have done a version of this exercise before, but perhaps never in this truly loving way - every day, Liz Gilbert writes a letter to herself from Love. A little bit like a conversation, without the judgement, advice, comparison or any requirement except to love — the kind of all encompassing comfort that we all need each day.

It may seem strange at first, so here's a few lines to get you started.

Start the conversation...
Dear Love, I need you...

Love responds...
Dear one I'm here, I never left you, I was always here, I will always be here.

Continue the conversation...
Love, today this is happening...

Love responds...
You are right where you need to be there is nowhere else you need to be, nothing else you need to be, do or have...

Dear Love,

SO CHERISHED

HOW MUCH TIME AND ENERGY DO YOU GIVE TO YOUR FAMILY AND FRIENDS?

....
....
....

NOW HOW MUCH TIME AND ENERGY DO YOU GIVE TO YOURSELF?

....
....
....

IS THERE A BIG DIFFERENCE?

....
....
....

WHAT ACTIVITIES CAN YOU DO TO STEP BACK AND TAKE CARE OF YOURSELF?

....
....
....
....
....

P.S. Self care doesn't have to mean a bubble bath and candles, it can be something as simple as taking a deep breath and practicing mindfulness, it could be going for a walk or spending the day in your PJs. Whatever recharges you and helps you feel good.

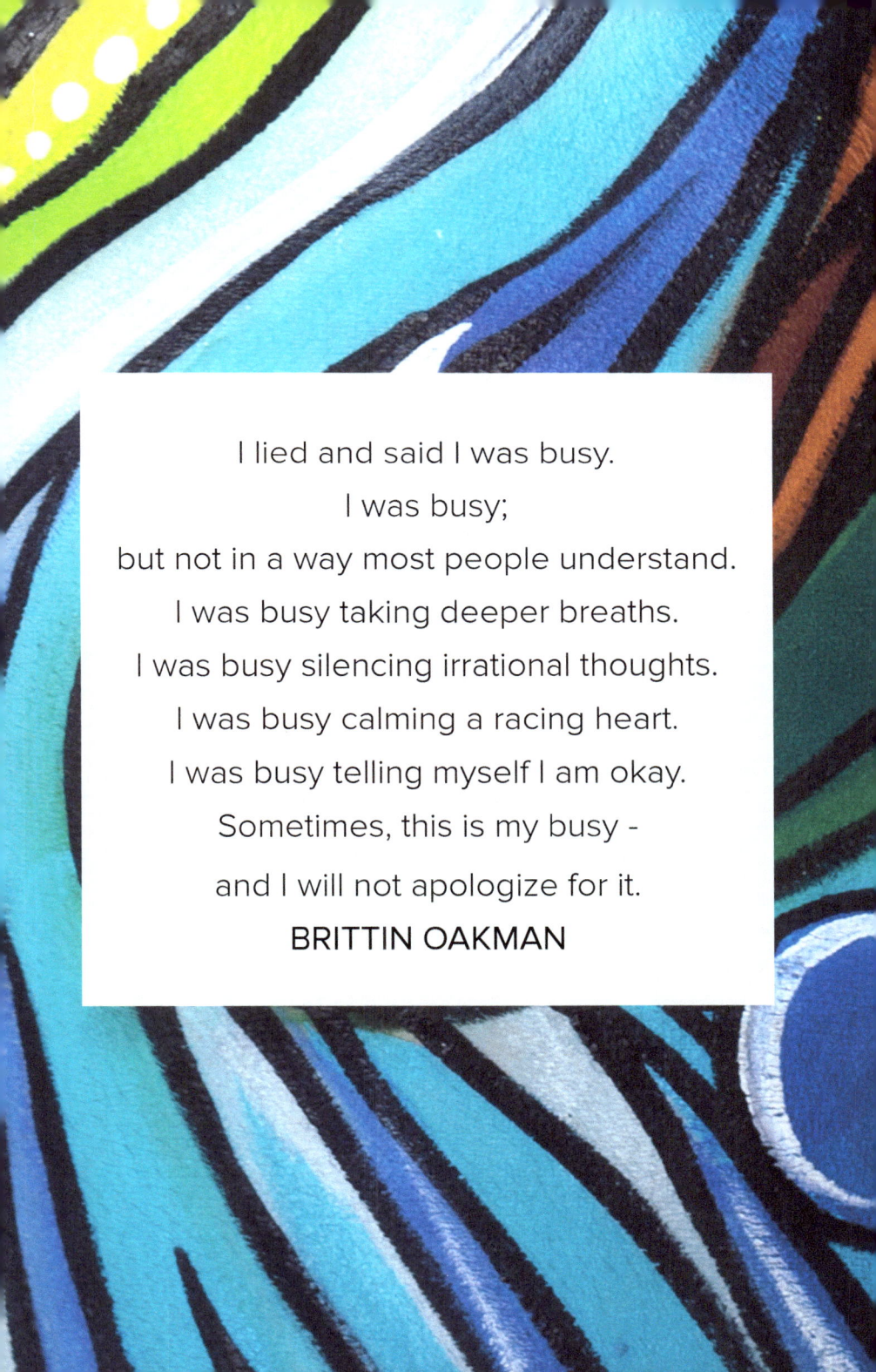

I lied and said I was busy.

I was busy;

but not in a way most people understand.

I was busy taking deeper breaths.

I was busy silencing irrational thoughts.

I was busy calming a racing heart.

I was busy telling myself I am okay.

Sometimes, this is my busy -

and I will not apologize for it.

BRITTIN OAKMAN

Let's try a breathing exercise

You can do this sitting down or standing up, however you are most comfortable.

Firstly, inhale through your nose slowly but deeply.

Feel your abdomen expand and your chest rise.

Then slowly exhale through your mouth.

Repeat this several times until you feel more relaxed.

How do you feel now?

In her footsteps

TAYLOR SWIFT

Being a pop sensation comes with its downfalls, Taylor has fallen victim to her fair share of trolls and bullies. She is known to speak to her haters through her songs like *"You Need to Calm Down"*. While her style of clapback might not come naturally to all of us, she is an inspiration to remember the best revenge is success. Cue *"Shake it off"*.

Taylor has her own toolbox to make sure she practices self-care. Whether that be adding things that she is looking forward to in her countdown app. Or reading words from Jameela Jamil as a voice of reason when it comes to the overwhelming expectations on women to defy gravity and time to look a certain way. Even so, one of her biggest lessons has come from accepting that trying and failing is just a part of life.

> "IT MAY NOT FEEL NORMAL TO ME BECAUSE ALL OF MY TRIALS AND FAILURES ARE BLOWN OUT OF PROPORTION AND TURNED INTO A SPECTATOR SPORT BY TABLOID TAKEDOWN CULTURE (YOU HAD TO GIVE ME ONE MOMENT OF BITTERNESS, COME ON). BUT THAT SAID, IT'S GOOD TO MESS UP AND LEARN FROM IT AND TAKE RISKS,"

WRITE DOWN A SONG LYRIC THAT BRINGS YOU JOY. WHILE YOU ARE AT IT WHY DON'T YOU PUT ON YOUR FAVOURITE PLAYLIST!

....

....

....

....

HOW DO YOU SHAKE OFF NEGATIVITY?

WHAT HAVE YOU LEARNT FROM MESSING UP?

Check in

WHAT DO I LIKE TO DO? REFLECT ON THE RESPONSES YOU USED IN THE GOALS 10 X 10 CHALLENGE.

....
....
....
....
....
....
....
....
....

WHEN WAS THE LAST TIME YOU DID ONE OF THOSE THINGS?

....
....
....

LET'S SCHEDULE SOME MORE OF THIS INTO YOUR DIARY —
HOW OFTEN CAN YOU DO THE TOP THREE THINGS ON YOUR LIST?

....
....
....
....

SO CHERISHED

HAVE YOU PRACTICED GRATITUDE AND MINDFULNESS LATELY?
....

TAKE A MOMENT TO THINK OF WHY YOU'RE GRATEFUL TODAY BY COMPLETING THE FOLLOWING: I'M GRATEFUL BECAUSE MY...

ME	1.	....
	2.	....
FAMILY	1.	....
	2.	....
FRIENDS	1.	....
	2.	....
HEALTH	1.	....
	2.	....
HOME	1.	....
	2.	....
WORK	1.	....
	2.	....
FOOD	1.	....
	2.	....
....	1.	....
	2.	....

HOW FAR DOWN THE LIST DO YOU GO BEFORE YOU THANK YOURSELF FOR ALL THE AMAZINGNESS THAT IS YOU?
....
....
....

In a society that says 'Put yourself last,' self-love and self-acceptance are almost revolutionary.

Brené Brown

So Mindful
Mental Health

Never be ashamed of what you feel.
You have the right to feel any emotion
that you want, and to do what makes
you happy. That's my life motto.

DEMI LOVATO

In her footsteps

DEMI LOVATO

Beloved for her Disney roles like Camp Rock and Sonny with a Chance, Demi Lovato quickly became a teen icon. Soon we heard her songs like *"Sorry Not Sorry"* and *"I Love Me"* playing on our radios. However, behind her brave face the singer has suffered with a bipolar disorder, multiple cases of addiction, depression and anxiety. She now uses her voice to bring awareness to mental health issues and her struggles with addiction. Unafraid to share her experiences, she has become living proof that it is still possible to live well with a mental illness.

"IF YOU'RE STRUGGLING AS WELL, DON'T FORGET...
IF I CAN DO IT, YOU CAN TOO!".

LIST 5 THINGS THAT YOU THINK WILL HELP TO UPLIFT YOU IN A MENTAL CRISIS (PEOPLE TO CALL, PLACES TO GO, THINGS TO DO).

YOU CAN USE THESE TO LOOK BACK ON.

1.
2.
3.
4.
5.

SO MINDFUL

WHEN WAS YOUR MENTAL HEALTH AT ITS BEST? WHY?

....
....
....
....
....

WHEN WAS YOUR MENTAL HEALTH AT ITS WORST? WHY?

....
....
....
....
....

FINISH THIS SENTENCE: RECENTLY I HAVE BEEN FEELING LIKE ...

....
....
....
....
....

HOW WOULD YOU RATE YOUR MENTAL HEALTH AT THE MOMENT?

For immediate help, call Lifeline on 13 11 14. If these questions have brought up any issues of concern, please reach out.

DO YOU KNOW WHEN YOUR MENTAL HEALTH IS DETERIORATING?

WHAT ARE THOSE WARNING SIGNS?

WHO DO YOU ASK FOR HELP?

DO YOU THINK YOUR MENTAL HEALTH SOMETIMES HOLDS YOU BACK?

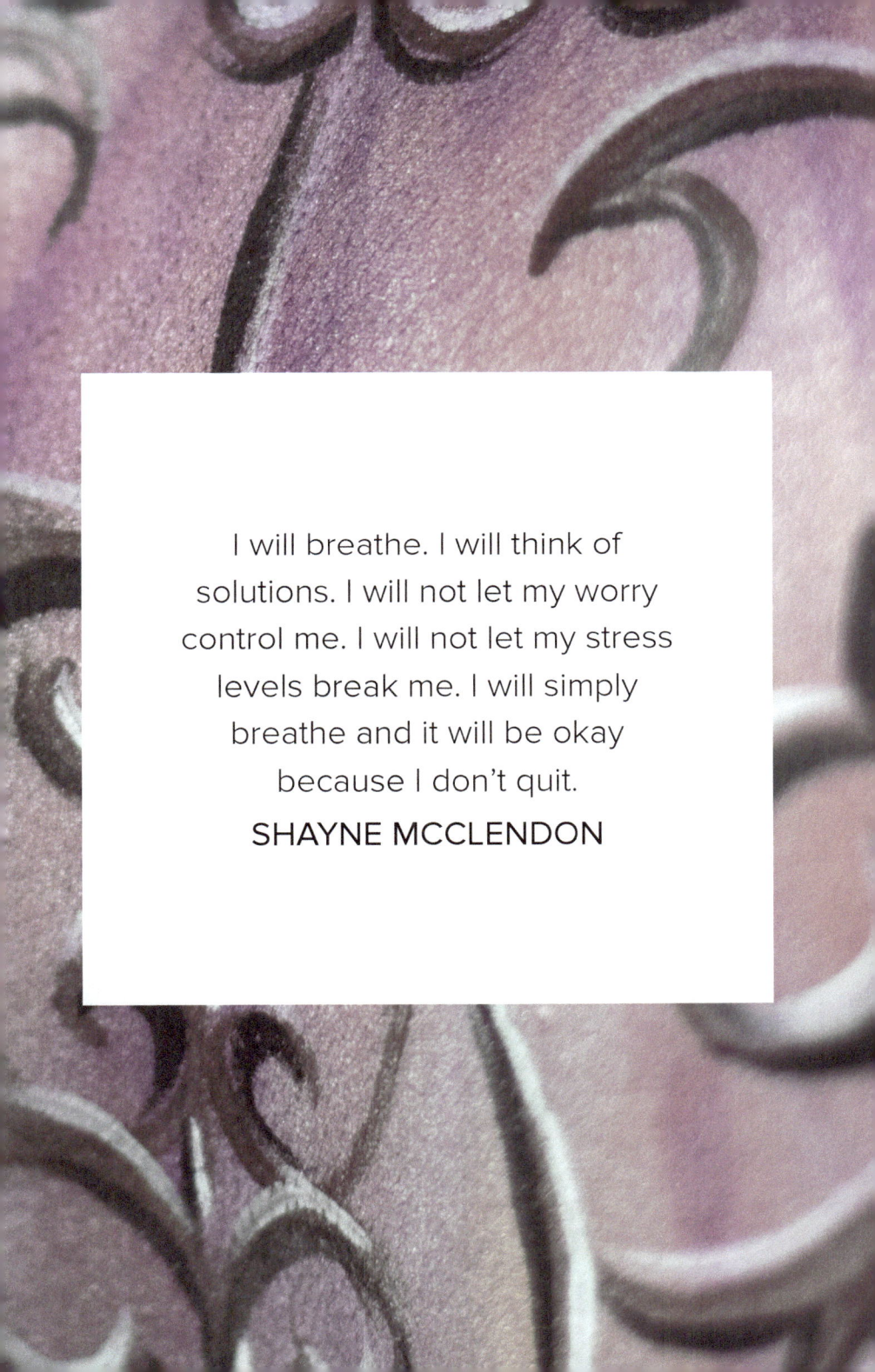

I will breathe. I will think of solutions. I will not let my worry control me. I will not let my stress levels break me. I will simply breathe and it will be okay because I don't quit.

SHAYNE MCCLENDON

Let worry tell you how it feels...

Similar to the *Letter to Love*, this exercise requires time and space, and can bring up some confronting ideas that have been bothering you conciously or sub-consciously for some time.

Allow your worry to personify and write you a letter about everything they're feeling – don't try and solve their problems, just let them speak.

Worry is like a rocking chair:
it gives you something to do
but never gets you anywhere.

ERMA BOMBECK

In her footsteps

GLENNON DOYLE

Glennon Doyle is a New York Times best-selling author. She struggled with bulimia for 18 years from the age of 8 and was sent to a mental hospital as a teen. In college she began her fall into alcoholism and drug use. Avoiding come down by bingeing and purging through the day, then booze, drugs and boys come nightfall.

> "BUT ON MOTHER'S DAY — ONE MOTHER'S DAY I FOUND MYSELF ON A COLD BATHROOM FLOOR, HUNG OVER, SHAKING AND HOLDING A POSITIVE PREGNANCY TEST. … AND SO THAT DAY ON THE BATHROOM FLOOR, I DECIDED TO SHOW UP. JUST TO SHOW UP, TO CLIMB OUT OF MY DARK INDIVIDUAL CONTROLLABLE WORLD AND OUT INTO THE BIG, BRIGHT, MESSY ONE."

Glennon, sober, went on to have three kids and now has a beautiful blended family. She has helped countless people get through some of the hardest times in their lives through her non-profit *Together Rising*.

> She is trying to be brave,
> but no one knows
> what brave looks like
> inside this particular moment.
>
> **GLENNON DOYLE**

Let's try a grounding exercise

Once you find your breath, go through the following steps to help ground yourself:

5: Acknowledge **FIVE** things you see around you.
4: Acknowledge **FOUR** things you can touch around you.
3: Acknowledge **THREE** things you hear.
2: Acknowledge **TWO** things you can smell.
1: Acknowledge **ONE** thing you can taste.

Daily Routines

Try to bring some of the following into your daily routine to help ease your stresses and clear your mind.

MINDFULNESS	EMOTIONAL RELEASE
meditation	journaling
yoga	talk to a friend
light candles	intense exercise
have a bath	change your environment
aromatherapy	tidy up your space
exercise	play your favourite tunes

Check in

FINISH THIS SENTENCE: MY KEY TAKE-AWAY FROM THIS MODULE IS ...

....
....
....
....
....
....

HAS YOUR VIEW ON THE IMPORTANCE OF MENTAL HEALTH CHANGED?

....
....
....
....
....
....
....
....
....
....
....
....
....

So Courageous
Self-Advocacy

You have the right to be involved. You have something important to contribute, and you have to take the risk to contribute it.

MAE JEMISON

In her footsteps

ELLEN DEGENERES

Ellen DeGeneres has become one of the most well-known comics on our TV today. Which can make it easy to forget how far she has come from her debut character, Ellen Morgan on the ABC sitcom, *Ellen*. In 1996, *Ellen* became the first prime time sitcom to feature a gay leading character. One-week prior Ellen made her own public "coming out" on the cover of the *Times*, displaying "Yep, I'm Gay". It took a lot of courage in a time where very few celebrities were openly gay and the few who were faced open discrimination. Ellen's entire life went into a tailspin as ABC, which cancelled *Ellen* a year after its historic high as ratings plummeted, and no one wanted to hire her. Years later, Ellen found a platform without the same prejudice – her self-titled talk show has now been running for nearly 2 decades and encourages viewers *to be kind to one another*. When asked about how she had the courage to open up to the world, DeGeneres discussed with Oprah that she had first felt that it was no one's business;

> "THEN I REALIZED THAT AS LONG AS I HAD THIS SECRET THAT I WORRIED ABOUT ALL THE TIME THAT IT MADE IT LOOK LIKE SOMETHING WAS WRONG."

Her resilience gave confidence to those who then followed in her footsteps and have come to make our television screens more inclusive today.

WHAT ARE YOU AFRAID TO TELL THE PEOPLE CLOSEST TO YOU ABOUT YOURSELF?

....

....

....

SO COURAGEOUS

WHAT DOES COURAGE MEAN TO YOU?

....
....
....
....
....

THINK OF A TIME WHEN YOU HAVE BEEN COURAGEOUS. WHAT DID YOU DO?

....
....
....
....
....

HOW DID IT FEEL?

....
....
....
....
....
....
....
....

SO COURAGEOUS

IF YOU HAD TO DESCRIBE YOURSELF, WHAT WORDS WOULD YOU USE?

....
....
....
....
....

REFLECT ON THESE LABELS - ARE THEY UPLIFTING, ARE THEY DEMEANING — HOW DO THESE WORDS LIFT YOU UP OR PULL YOU BACK?

....
....
....
....

TRY DESCRIBING YOURSELF AS OTHERS SEE YOU. HOW DOES THIS DIFFER?

....
....
....
....

WHAT YOU TELL YOURSELF EVERYDAY WILL EITHER LIFT YOU UP OR TEAR YOU DOWN

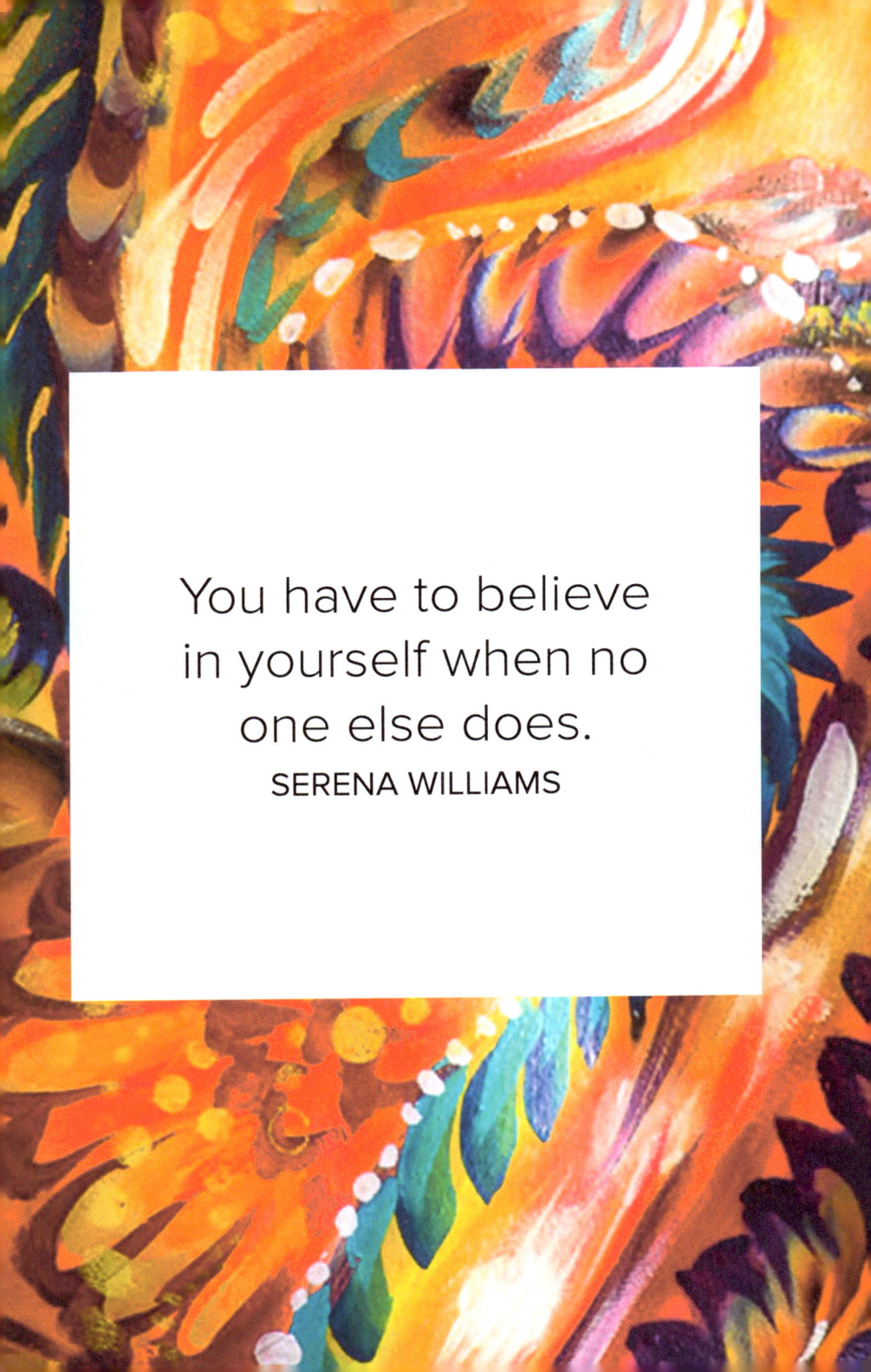

You have to believe in yourself when no one else does.
SERENA WILLIAMS

In her footsteps

REESE WITHERSPOON

After being sick of the lack of diversity in female roles in films, American actress, Reese Witherspoon, took the issue into her own hands and started her own company, *Pacific Standard Films*. While being told that there wasn't a market for buying female driven material. After sifting through manuscripts, she put her beliefs and her own money into two pieces of material. Both based on strong, complex women and also written by women. *Gone Girl* and *Wild* made over half a billion dollars worldwide and both films becoming Oscar-nominated. Although we still see a lack of representation of women, whether that be in films or leadership positions. Reese encourages women to go after what people have said you cannot do and prove them wrong!

WRITE DOWN SOMETHING YOU HAVE ACHIEVED WHEN YOU WERE TOLD YOU COULDN'T.

SO COURAGEOUS

HAVE YOU FELT YOU WEREN'T SEEN/HEARD IN YOUR JOB? WRITE DOWN WHAT HAPPENED AND HOW YOU MANAGED THE SITUATION.

....
....
....
....
....
....
....

IF YOU WERE TO TAKE A STEP BACK FROM YOUR WORKPLACE, WHAT ARE THE CULTURE AND DYNAMICS THAT YOU'RE WORKING WITHIN? HOW CAN YOU CHANGE YOUR PERCEPTION OF WHAT IS HAPPENING?

....
....
....
....
....
....
....
....

Each time a woman stands up for herself,
she stands up for all women.

MAYA ANGELOU

WHAT STRATEGIES CAN YOU LEVERAGE TO IMPROVE YOUR ABILITY TO BE SEEN AND HEARD IN YOUR WORKPLACE?

....
....
....
....
....

WHO CAN YOU TALK TO ABOUT THIS IN YOUR WORKPLACE? DO YOU HAVE ALLIES OR MENTORS?

....
....
....
....
....

THINK ABOUT YOUR WORKPLACE OR UNIVERSITY OR CHURCH, WHAT'S THE DIVERSITY OF PEOPLE IN LEADERSHIP POSITIONS LIKE?

....
....
....
....
....
....
....
....

> The question isn't who's going to let me; it's who is going to stop me.
>
> — AYN RAND

In her footsteps

MALALA

Malala first spoke out for girls' education when she was just a child herself. When the Taliban started attacking girls' schools, she gave a speech, titled "How dare the Taliban take away my basic right to education?". When she was only 11 years old, she began blogging for the BBC, her platform grew as she continued to fight for her right and the right of all women to an education. Soon after she learned that the Taliban had issued her death warrant.

Fifteen-year-old Malala rode the bus home from school when a masked gun man fired at her. Hitting her on the left side of the head leaving her in critical condition. Malala survived. Not only did she survive but she continues to fight for all women's right to education and became the youngest person ever to receive a Nobel Peace Prize at the age of 17. She has since launched the Malala fund which works to ensure girls have free and safe access to 12 years of education.

WHAT GLOBAL ISSUES DO YOU FEEL PASSIONATE ABOUT?

Ground-breaking Women

Dr Fiona Wood: Australian plastic surgeon who invented "spray-on skin" technology for use in treating burn victims.

Gloria Steinem: Leader in the 60's and 70's feminist movement.

Amelia Earheart: The first woman to fly solo across the Atlantic.

Jessica Watson: an Australian sailor who is the youngest person to sail solo and unassisted around the world at the age of 16.

Margaret Hamilton: Hand wrote the code that got man on the moon and safely back again.

Valentina Tereshkova: Former textile worker became the first woman in space at 26.

Coco Chanel: Challenged gender norms and redefined traditional women's fashion.

Melanie Perkins: Australian technology entrepreneur and one of the youngest female CEOs to be leading a tech startup valued at over a billion dollars.

WHAT ARE SOME ISSUES THAT YOU'RE PASSIONATE ABOUT ON A LOCAL LEVEL?

RECOGNISING HOW FAR YOU'VE COME SOMETIMES STARTS WITH RECOGNISING THE LEGACY WE'VE BEEN BORN INTO.
WHAT ARE YOU GRATEFUL TO THE WOMEN WHO CAME BEFORE US FOR?

> The most effective way to do it, is to do it.
> — AMELIA EARHART

Check in

HAVE YOU SHOWN MORE COURAGE RECENTLY?

HOW DID IT MAKE YOU FEEL?

WHAT WAS THE OUTCOME?

So Savvy
Financial Fitness

Financial independence is paramount. My mom always says that when a woman is financially independent, she has the ability to live life on her own terms.

PRIYANKA CHOPRA

In her footsteps

JENNIFER LAWRENCE

If Academy and Oscar winning actress Jennifer Lawrence, one of the highest paid actresses in the world, still has difficulty speaking up for her basic right to equal pay in this day and age, you can bet there will be situations where the rest of us will also doubt fighting for ourselves. Jennifer only found out she was paid considerably less than her male co-stars in the film *American Hustle* after Sony was hacked and the information was leaked. Whilst long being silent on such issues, she wrote an essay for feminist newsletter, *Lenny*, about how her fear of being difficult stopped her from fighting and asking for more money.

> "I'M OVER TRYING TO FIND THE 'ADORABLE' WAY TO STATE MY OPINION AND STILL BE LIKABLE! F*CK THAT. I DON'T THINK I'VE EVER WORKED FOR A MAN IN CHARGE WHO SPENT TIME CONTEMPLATING WHAT ANGLE HE SHOULD USE TO HAVE HIS VOICE HEARD. IT'S JUST HEARD."

Remember your worth and don't sell yourself short.

IF YOU WERE UNAFRAID WHAT WOULD YOU ASK FOR TODAY?

WHAT ARE SOME OF YOUR FINANCIAL GOALS?

HOW DO YOU FEEL WHEN IT COMES TO DISCUSSING YOUR WAGE/SALARY?

HOW DO YOU FEEL ABOUT MONEY? FINISH THIS SENTENCE: MY RELATIONSHIP WITH MONEY IS.....

CHANGING YOUR MINDSET ABOUT MONEY IS VERY IMPORTANT — IF MONEY AND YOU WERE BEST FRIENDS, HOW WOULD YOU TALK ABOUT IT?

Financial fitness exercise

Do you know how much you've got in savings and how much you owe right now?

ACCOUNT .... $ .... (OWING / SAVINGS)

ACCOUNT .... $ .... (OWING / SAVINGS)

ACCOUNT .... $ .... (OWING / SAVINGS)

ACCOUNT .... $ .... (OWING / SAVINGS)

....

....

....

Think about what you want to **be**, **do** and **have** in your life...

Make a list against each of these and write one step you can take today to make that happen.

BE

DO

HAVE

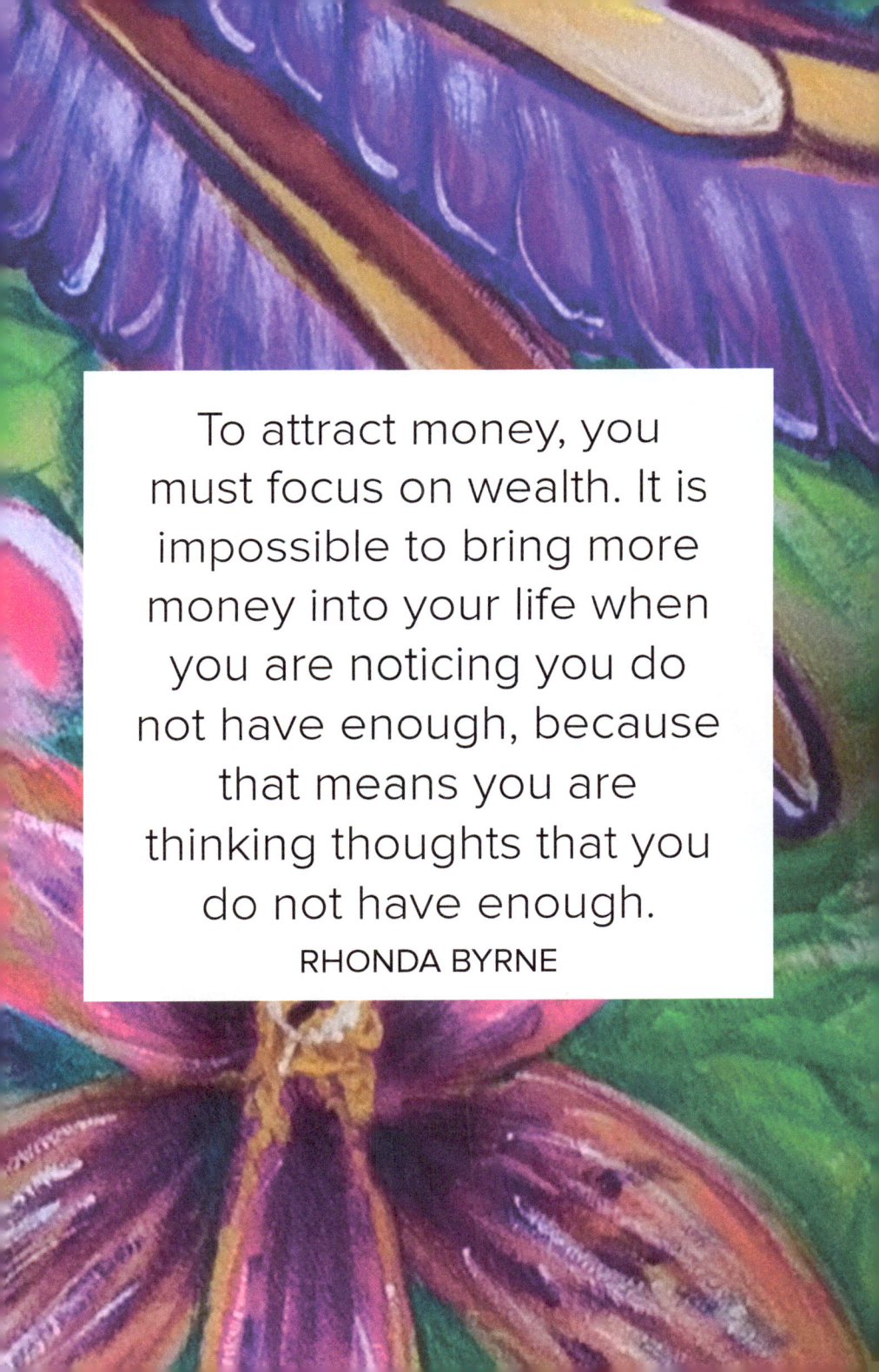

> To attract money, you must focus on wealth. It is impossible to bring more money into your life when you are noticing you do not have enough, because that means you are thinking thoughts that you do not have enough.
>
> RHONDA BYRNE

The story of my life

IF YOU WROTE YOUR OWN SCRIPT FOR HOW YOUR LIFE STORY WAS TO GO, WHAT WOULD IT LOOK LIKE?

SO SAVVY

You can be the lead in your own life.

KERRY WASHINGTON

In her footsteps

TIFFANY HADISH

At three years old Tiffany's father left. When she was eight, she became the de facto parent for her four siblings after her mother was left with a brain injury due to a car accident which later turned into mental illness. At age thirteen she ended up in foster care, separated from her siblings. By age fifteen she had not learned to read beyond a first-grade level. Her resulting "behavioural issues" had a social worker take notice of how she could make her classmates laugh and sent her to a comedy camp.

In her twenties she worked multiple jobs and lived in her car while trying to make a career in comedy. She used her life as material and finally had her first break on a comedy competition show *Who's Got Jokes*. At age 37 after several smaller comedic acting roles she finally had her breakout performance on *Girls Trip*, starring alongside Jada Pinkett Smith, Queen Latifah and Regina Hall. Tiffany — a stand-up comedienne — became a global sensation, securing her own comedy special and became the first female African-American female to host *Saturday Night Live*. She now hopes to set up a community centre for young people in foster care, as she once was.

HOW CAN YOU GIVE BACK?

Help us create a legacy for the next generation of young women — ⭐ donate now ⭐ sobrave.com.au/donate

Especially as women, we are pressured to achieve certain milestones by a certain age. Whether that be establishing your career and getting married in your twenties, to buying a house and having kids before you are thirty.

Remember we are all on our own journey!

WHERE 'SHOULD' YOU BE AT 'YOUR STAGE' OF LIFE?
WHAT ARE YOUR THOUGHTS ABOUT THIS?

Budgeting your money is the key to having enough.
ELIZABETH WARREN

WHAT BIG EXPENSES ARE COMING UP IN THE NEXT 10 YEARS?

....
....
....
....

HOW CAN YOU START PLANNING FOR THEM NOW?

....
....
....
....
....
....

IT'S TIME TO LOOK AT WHERE YOU'RE AT RIGHT NOW: WHAT'S HOLDING YOU BACK RIGHT NOW?

....
....
....
....

HOW CAN YOU LET GO OF WHAT IS HOLDING YOU BACK?

....
....
....
....
....

Check in

LET'S DO A FINANCIAL HEALTH CHECK

DO YOU KNOW IF YOU HAVE SUPER – IF SO, HOW MUCH AND HOW MANY ACCOUNTS DO YOU HAVE? DO YOU KNOW WHAT FEES YOU'RE PAYING?

....
....
....
....
....

HAVE YOU CONSIDERED INSURANCES – CAR, HEALTH, LIFE, TRAUMA, INCOME PROTECTION?

....
....
....
....
....

CHECK YOUR SUPER AS YOU MAY HAVE SOME COVERAGE, BUT HAVE YOU THOUGHT ABOUT WHETHER IT'S ENOUGH AND WHAT OTHER NEEDS YOU HAVE?

....
....
....
....
....

INVESTING AND DEBT – WHERE ARE YOU NOW WITH YOUR FINANCES?

DO YOU HAVE A GOOD IDEA OF HOW MUCH DEBT OR SAVINGS YOU HAVE?

DO YOU KNOW HOW MUCH YOU NEED IN YOUR SUPER TO LIVE WELL IN YOUR RETIREMENT? DO SOME BASIC CALCULATIONS - THE FIGURE MAY SURPRISE YOU!

Did you know billions of dollars is held in unclaimed super?!

Searching for lost super? Call 13 28 65

So Confident

Self-Esteem and Confidence

Don't fall into the trap of sacrificing your self-esteem for affection and acceptance. No matter what your size, you are a sexy goddess. Remember that.

ASHLEY GRAHAM

In her footsteps

LIZZO

Lizzo is the queen of self-love anthems. She inspires fans every day to love themselves. But she didn't always even love herself.

She has shared that growing up she wanted to change everything about herself. The lack of representation in the media made her feel as if the world was telling her she wasn't lovable. Her self-hatred escalated so far that she wanted to be other people, until she realised you can't live trying to be someone else.

"LOVING MYSELF WAS THE RESULT OF ANSWERING TWO THINGS: DO YOU WANT TO LIVE? 'CAUSE THIS IS WHO YOU'RE GONNA BE FOR THE REST OF YOUR LIFE. OR ARE YOU GONNA JUST HAVE A LIFE OF EMPTINESS, SELF-HATRED AND SELF-LOATHING? AND I CHOSE TO LIVE, SO I HAD TO ACCEPT MYSELF. THAT'S THE FIRST STEP: ACCEPTANCE. AND ACCEPTANCE IS HARD. I'M STILL ACCEPTING MYSELF EVERY DAY; I'M STILL WORKING ON IT."

Look up in the mirror like,
DAMN SHE THE ONE.

LIZZO, *SOULMATE*

IF YOU WERE TO LOOK IN THE MIRROR, WHAT WOULD YOU BE SAYING TO YOURSELF?

LIZZO PUT OUT THIS CHALLENGE TO HER FANS ON INSTAGRAM. HAVE A GO!

Can you do me a HUGE favor?

No matter what you're doing right now.
Can you take a second and pause?

Now take 3 deep breaths...

1 ... 2 ... and a super deep breath on 3.....

Imagine pure love coming into your body and hold it right on your heart. Then say to yourself: "I LOVE YOU. YOU ARE BEAUTIFUL. AND YOU CAN DO ANYTHING."

Repeat as many times as you need.

SO CONFIDENT

WHAT IS YOUR FAVOURITE THING ABOUT YOURSELF?

....

....

....

WRITE OUT YOUR NAME AND FOR EACH LETTER WRITE DOWN ONE WORD YOU WOULD USE TO DESCRIBE YOURSELF.

E.G. SAM – SUPPORTIVE, ASSERTIVE, MAGNANIMOUS

....

....

....

....

....

....

NAME FIVE QUALITIES YOU ADMIRE IN OTHERS:

1. ....
2. ....
3. ....
4. ....
5. ....

HOW DO YOU SEE THESE QUALITIES REFLECTED IN YOURSELF?

....

....

....

....

....

Always find a reason to laugh.

It may not add years to your life but it will add life to your years.

SO CONFIDENT

In her footsteps

PINK

"RECENTLY, I WAS DRIVING MY DAUGHTER TO SCHOOL AND SHE SAID TO ME, OUT OF THE BLUE, 'MAMA?' I SAID, 'YES, BABY?' SHE SAID, 'I'M THE UGLIEST GIRL I KNOW.' AND I SAID, 'HUH?' AND SHE WAS LIKE, 'YEAH, I LOOK LIKE A BOY WITH LONG HAIR.' AND MY BRAIN WENT TO OH MY GOD, YOU'RE 6. WHY? WHERE IS THIS COMING FROM? WHO SAID THIS? CAN I KICK A 6-YEAR-OLD'S ASS, LIKE WHAT?"

"BUT I DIDN'T SAY ANYTHING. INSTEAD I WENT HOME AND I MADE A POWERPOINT PRESENTATION FOR HER. AND IN THAT PRESENTATION WERE ANDROGYNOUS ROCKSTARS AND ARTISTS THAT LIVE THEIR TRUTH, ARE PROBABLY MADE FUN OF EVERY DAY OF THEIR LIFE, AND CARRY ON, WAVE THEIR FLAG, AND INSPIRE THE REST OF US. AND THESE ARE ARTISTS LIKE MICHAEL JACKSON AND DAVID BOWIE AND FREDDIE MERCURY AND ANNIE LENNOX AND PRINCE AND JANIS JOPLIN AND GEORGE MICHAEL, ELTON JOHN, SO MANY ARTISTS — HER EYES GLAZED OVER. BUT THEN I SAID, 'YOU KNOW, I REALLY WANNA KNOW WHY YOU FEEL THIS WAY ABOUT YOURSELF.' AND SHE SAID, 'WELL I LOOK LIKE A BOY,' AND I SAID, 'WELL WHAT DO YOU THINK I LOOK LIKE?' AND SHE SAID, 'WELL YOU'RE BEAUTIFUL.' AND I WAS LIKE, 'WELL, THANKS. BUT WHEN PEOPLE MAKE FUN OF ME, THAT'S WHAT THEY USE. THEY SAY I LOOK LIKE A BOY OR I'M TOO MASCULINE OR I HAVE TOO MANY OPINIONS, MY BODY IS TOO STRONG.'"

"AND I SAID TO HER, 'DO YOU SEE ME GROWING MY HAIR?' SHE SAID, 'NO, MAMA.' I SAID, 'DO YOU SEE ME CHANGING MY BODY?' 'NO, MAMA.' 'DO YOU SEE ME CHANGING THE WAY I PRESENT MYSELF TO THE WORLD?' 'NO, MAMA.' 'DO YOU SEE ME SELLING OUT ARENAS ALL OVER THE WORLD?' 'YES, MAMA.' 'OK! SO, BABY GIRL. WE DON'T CHANGE. WE TAKE THE GRAVEL AND THE SHELL AND WE MAKE A PEARL. AND WE HELP OTHER PEOPLE TO CHANGE SO THEY CAN SEE MORE KINDS OF BEAUTY.'"

2017 MTV VMA's Speech

SO CONFIDENT

HOW ARE YOU BRINGING YOUR KIND OF BEAUTY TO THE WORLD?

....

....

....

....

HOW CAN YOU SHARE THIS WITH OTHERS?

....

....

....

....

....

WHO DECIDES HOW YOU FEEL AND HOW AMAZING YOU ARE?

....

....

....

....

....

DEFINE CONFIDENCE:

....

....

....

....

....

....

Don't you ever let a soul in the world tell you that you can't be exactly who you are.
LADY GAGA

Write your perfect day

Where did you wake up? What did you have for breakfast? Did you have a shower, or go for a swim? What did you do in the morning? What did you have for lunch? Who did you have lunch with? How did you spend your afternoon? What did you do into the evening? What did you do before going to bed and when did you finish your day?

Check in

HOW ARE YOU DOING TODAY?

....
....
....
....
....

HOW HAS YOUR CONFIDENCE GROWN?

....
....
....
....
....
....
....

HOW HAVE YOU CHANGED THE WAY YOU VIEW YOURSELF?

....
....
....
....
....
....
....

So Healthy
Health and Wellness

Just believe in yourself.
Even if you don't,
PRETEND that you do and,
at some point, you will.

VENUS WILLIAMS

In her footsteps

ASHLEY GRAHAM

You could think that 'plus size' models are eating whatever they want and don't get off the couch. That is definitely not the case. Ashley Graham, the first ever size 14 model on the cover of *Sports Illustrated*, not only works hard at shattering body stereotypes but also at the gym. She maintains a healthy lifestyle nourishing and moving her body. While she makes working out a priority in her life, she voices that she does it to stay healthy, feel good and clear her mind, not to lose weight or try to get thin.

> 'I'VE DONE EVERY YO-YO DIET YOU CAN IMAGINE AND NONE WORK FOR ME. I'M AT A COMFORTABLE WEIGHT AND I KNOW THAT I LOOK GOOD AND, MORE IMPORTANTLY, I FEEL GOOD SO WHY AM I DIETING?'

HOW DO YOU LISTEN TO YOUR BODY?

WHAT IS YOUR RELATIONSHIP WITH EXERCISE? DO YOU LOVE IT? HATE IT?

WHY DO YOU/DON'T YOU DO IT?

YOU CAN DO IT!

SO HEALTHY

AFTER EXERCISING I FEEL ....

....
....
....
....
....
....
....
....

WHAT IS YOUR FAVOURITE 'HEALTHY' THING TO DO?

....
....
....
....
....

WHAT ARE FIVE WAYS YOU COULD BE MORE ACTIVE EVERY DAY?

1. ....
2. ....
3. ....
4. ....
5. ....

Think about introducing these into your everyday routine.

SO HEALTHY

Rate yourself

HOW MANY GLASSES OF WATER DO YOU DRINK PER DAY?

I NEED TO INCREASE: YES   /   NO

HOW MANY DAYS PER WEEK DO YOU GET YOUR 5 SERVES OF FRUIT/VEG?

I NEED TO INCREASE: YES   /   NO

HOW MANY HOURS OF SLEEP DO YOU GET EACH NIGHT?

I NEED TO: INCREASE   /   DEACREASE

HOW OFTEN YOU GET TAKE AWAY PER WEEK?

I NEED TO DECREASE: YES   /   NO

HOW MANY GLASSES OF ALCOHOL DO YOU DRINK PER WEEK?

I NEED TO DECREASE: YES   /   NO

It's never too late
to change old habits.
FLORENCE GRIFFITH JOYNER

In her footsteps

GAL GADOT

As the all powerful Wonder Woman, Gal Gadot needed more than her natural athleticism and beauty to get into shape for the part. She explains that training for the first film was "a lot more intensive" than her time in the Israeli army - training for six hours a day for six months prior to shooting.

> "I DID TWO HOURS GYM WORK, TWO HOURS FIGHT CHOREOGRAPHY AND ONE AND A HALF HOURS—TWO HOURS HORSEBACK RIDING, WHICH IS SUPER HARD! WHEN PEOPLE USED TO TELL ME, 'YEAH, I DO SPORT, I RIDE HORSES,' I WAS LIKE, 'THAT'S NOT SPORT, THE HORSE DOES EVERYTHING.' BUT NO! YOU'LL BE SURPRISED, IT'S SO PAINFUL."

Sometimes it feels like the world is expecting us to be some sort of Wonder Woman. First, you have to get good grades if you want to excel in your career. But you also must focus on having a good social life to share on Instagram, you don't want to seem like a total bookworm. All whilst looking after your family, being happy, not stressed, making sure your make up is done, but not too much, eating right and maintaining the perfect slim, toned body.

There are so many unrealistic expectations placed on how women's bodies should look. Many young Australian girls grew up playing with Barbies. Idealising her as having the perfect body. If Barbie was scaled to the height of an average woman, her waist would be around 50 centimetres compared to 90 centimetres for the average Australian woman.

While it is incredibly important to look after your body for your own health and wellbeing, remember that health is unique to every individual.

WHAT IS YOUR VISION OF HEALTH AND WELLNESS?

WHAT WOULD YOU NEED TO CHANGE FOR THIS VISION TO BECOME REALITY?

HOW DO YOU FEEL ABOUT FOOD?

HOW DO YOU THINK YOUR CURRENT DIET WILL AFFECT YOUR BODY IN THE FUTURE?

HOW DOES YOUR LIFESTYLE IMPACT YOUR FOOD CHOICES?

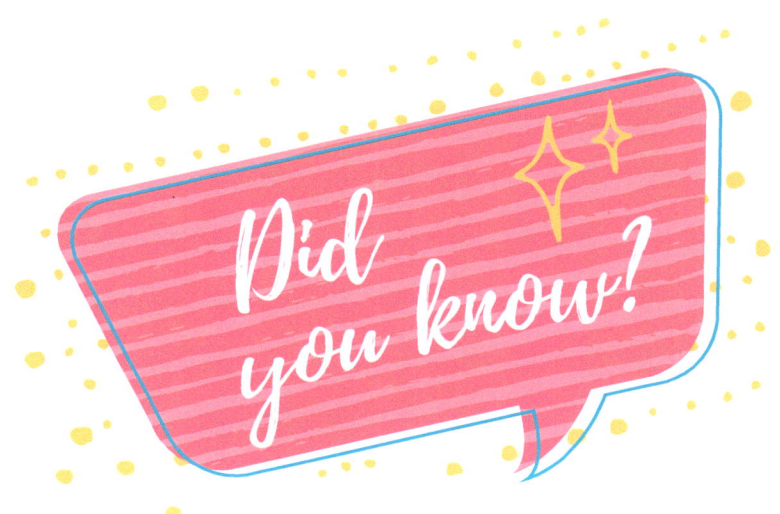

Keeping fit, eating well and having a healthy lifestyle helps to reduce the risk of developing breast cancer.

Moderate alcohol consumption (as many as three alcoholic drinks per week or more) has been linked to a higher risk of breast cancer.

Check in

HAS YOUR VIEW ON HEALTH AND WELLNESS CHANGED? HOW?

....
....
....
....
....
....

WHAT HAVE YOU CHANGED ABOUT YOUR ROUTINE?

....
....
....
....
....
....

HOW DO YOU FEEL BETTER?

....
....
....
....
....
....

So Powerful
Sexual Health

Boy, girl, man, or woman— "No means No"!
It could be a "Yes" yesterday, but a "No"
today. And that's perfectly valid.

TINA SEQUEIRA

In her footsteps

LADY GAGA

> "BECAUSE OF THE WAY THAT I DRESS, AND THE WAY THAT I'M PROVOCATIVE AS A PERSON, I THOUGHT THAT I HAD BROUGHT IT ON MYSELF IN SOME WAY, THAT IT WAS MY FAULT. I DIDN'T KNOW HOW NOT TO BLAME MYSELF, OR THINK IT WAS MY FAULT. IT WAS SOMETHING THAT REALLY CHANGED MY LIFE. IT CHANGED WHO I WAS COMPLETELY."

A victim of assault is never to blame. No matter how they were acting or what they were wearing.

Lady Gaga is a singer, songwriter, actress, businesswoman, an advocate for LGBTQ+ rights and a sexual assault survivor. The shame she felt from the incident stopped her from opening up until years later and resulting in her suffering from PTSD. She has since aimed to stand by those who have suffered sexual assault, educate about mental illness caused by violence and expose the truth about sexual abuse in universities all over America.

Speaking openly about these issues and learning about topics such as consent can help make a difference.

> We must send a message across the world that there is no disgrace in being a survivor of sexual violence – the shame is on the aggressor.
>
> **ANGELINA JOLIE**

CONSIDER STARTING A CONVERSATION WITH YOURSELF ABOUT SEX:

Do I know what the other person wants?

Am I doing what I really want to do?

Am I looking forward to it?

Am I doing it because I'm frightened they'll be angry if I say no?

I'm not doing it because it's expected of me. Am I doing something because I think it's what I have to do?

Just because I've done something before, doesn't mean I have to do it again.

Do I feel able to talk about using condoms and/or contraception?

Am I sober? Are they sober?

Do we have a safe place to be with each other?

Adapted from the Griffith University booklet, *Love, Sex and Dating*

HOW WOULD YOU DESCRIBE CONSENT?

SO POWERFUL

WHAT DOES BEING A WOMAN MEAN TO YOU?

HAVE YOU EVER FELT 'LESS-THAN' BECAUSE OF YOUR GENDER OR SEXUALITY?

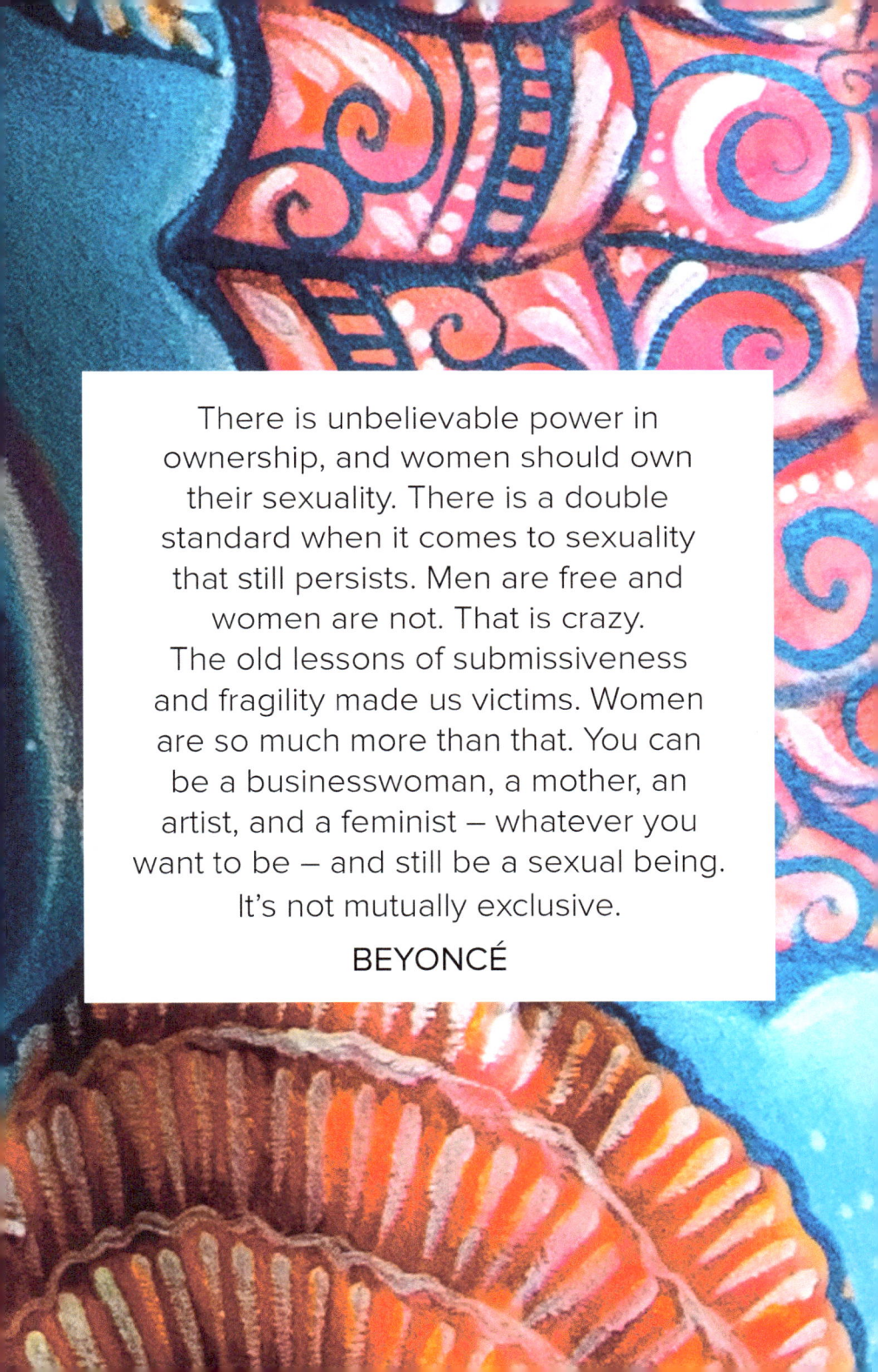

> There is unbelievable power in ownership, and women should own their sexuality. There is a double standard when it comes to sexuality that still persists. Men are free and women are not. That is crazy.
> The old lessons of submissiveness and fragility made us victims. Women are so much more than that. You can be a businesswoman, a mother, an artist, and a feminist — whatever you want to be — and still be a sexual being. It's not mutually exclusive.
>
> **BEYONCÉ**

My body is precious and not separate from my soul.

SARK

REGULAR HEALTH CHECKS FOR WOMEN

Good sexual health includes being aware of how to protect yourself and your sexual partners from sexually transmissible infections, seeking testing and treatment if you do get a sexually transmitted infection (STI), and having access to contraception.

In Australia:

- about 16% of Australians report having a sexually transmitted infection in their lifetime
- over 23,000 Australians are living with Human Immunodeficiency Virus (HIV)

So Brave recommends that you practice breast aware self checks and consult your doctor if you notice any unusual breast changes.

In addition to breast checks, the following regular health checks should be incorporated throughout your life:

20s and 30s:

- a Cervical Screening Test every five years after you turn 25
- a skin check from your doctor if you notice any changes to your skin that may indicate skin cancer
- a dental check-up as often as advised by your dentist
- an eye health test as often as advised by your optometrist
- vaccinations as needed for travel and boosters, and the yearly influenza shot
- a sexual health check at least once a year if you're sexually active, or if you think you might have an STI or have had unsafe sex
- vulvar health check
- regular blood pressure and cholesterol checks by your doctor
- regular breast checks

Add the following checks as you age:

40s

- you are eligible for free mammography screenings every two years (differs by state) with BreastScreen

50s +

- Most women can expect menopause to start during their 50s
- a bowel cancer screening test every two years
- bone density test as advised by your doctor

Queensland Department of Health and Australian Department of Health

WHAT ARE SOME ESSENTIAL HEALTH CHECKS FOR YOU?

....

....

....

In her footsteps

LENA DUNHAM

Lena Dunham is known for her starring role in the HBO series *Girls*. She uses her platform to create an open dialogue about issues surrounding women's health like periods and her experience with endometriosis.

Her first period was like many other women's experiences, awkward. On a father-daughter sunset hike she felt something trickling down her leg. Her first reaction thinking that she had peed herself. Realising it was blood she suspected a fatal injury. Her father looked at her and said "This, this mountain, is where we were the moment you became a woman. In many cultures you'd have to start birthing children now." After rushing home embarrassed, her father taught her through the crack in the door how to insert a tampon for the first time.

Lena describes that from her first period something didn't feel right. Some of her symptoms included severe cramps and long periods. Endometriosis symptoms can also include heavy flow, nausea, vomiting, pain during sex, infertility and more. Lena continues to share her story to reduce the stigma surrounding periods saying,

> "WE DON'T HAVE TO SNEAK TO THE BATHROOM WITH A PURSE ANYMORE."

HAS SOMETHING LIKE THIS HAPPENED TO YOU?

SO POWERFUL

DO YOU TRACK YOUR CYCLE?   YES   /   NO

DO YOU KNOW WHAT IS CONSIDERED NORMAL SURROUNDING PERIODS? CONSIDER TRACKING YOUR CYCLE FOR THE NEXT FEW MONTHS TO UNDERSTAND WHAT IS NORMAL FOR YOU.

....
....
....
....
....
....

HOW DO YOU STAY IN TUNE WITH YOUR BODY?

....
....
....
....
....

It is strange how little talk there is about our periods, as if the subject, if not in a health and wellness context were morally reprehensible. ... But why are we secretive? Over half the world menstruates at one time or another, and you'd never know it. Isn't that strange?

MARGARET CHO

Are you 25 or over?

If you are, it is well and truly time to book in for your pap smear, or as they're now known, cervical screening.

WHAT IS A CERVICAL SCREENING?

The Australian Medical Board recommends that all women book a cervical screening once they turn 25. If the screening shows no abnormalities, they will not be required to book another screening for five years unless they show symptoms.

A cervical screening is a procedure performed by your GP, it's quick, routine and shouldn't be too uncomfortable. Your doctor will insert a speculum inside your vagina, take a swap of your cervix and send the swap to a lab to test for human papillomavirus (HPV). HPV often clears on its own but it can cause cancer so it is important for your GP or gynecologist to monitor it.

WHY SHOULD YOU DO IT?

Thanks to the cervical screening, cervical cancer is one of the most preventable cancers. If you ensure you have your screening when recommended and keep an eye out for symptoms you are on track to stay accountable for your cervical health.

Australia leads the world in preventing cervical cancer through our human papillomavirus (HPV) vaccination program, however, even if you have had the vaccination, it is important to continue monitoring and surveillance throughout your lifetime. If in doubt, check it out.

Adapted from Get Papped and the Australian Department of Health.

YOUR ENDOMETRIOSIS CHECKLIST

Only a gynaecologist can diagnose you with endometriosis; however, there are a number of questions you can ask yourself to help you and your doctor understand what might be happening in your body.

Here are some important questions to ask yourself:

- ✓ How long does my period pain last?
- ✓ Is my period heavy?
- ✓ How severe is my pain?
- ✓ Where is the pain?
- ✓ Do over-the-counter painkillers relieve the pain?
- ✓ Does the pain stop me from doing regular activities?
- ✓ Are there any other symptoms I feel are not normal?

Make note of your answers and take this information along with you when you speak to your doctor.

The QENDO support line is also here to help you.

www.qendo.org.au | 1800 ASK QENDO | search "QENDO" on the app or goggle play store

Check in

WHAT DID YOU LEARN ABOUT YOUR BODY?

....
....
....
....
....
....

DOES YOUR FAMILY HAVE A *HER*STORY OF 'WOMEN'S ISSUES'?

....
....
....
....
....
....

WHO ELSE DO YOU NEED TO CONSULT FOR FURTHER INFORMATION?

....
....
....
....
....
....

Final Wrap Up
Towards bravery and resilience

Keep on beginning and failing.
Each time you fail, start all over again,
and you will grow stronger until you
have accomplished a purpose — not the
one you began with perhaps, but one
you'll be glad to remember.

ANNE SULLIVAN

So Focused

NOW THAT YOU KNOW YOURSELF A LITTLE BIT BETTER, WHAT'S YOUR BIG AUDACIOUS GOAL AND WHAT ARE THE STEPS YOU'RE TAKING TO ACHIEVE IT?

....

....

So Aware

HAVE YOU DONE YOUR MONTHLY BREAST CHECK, AND IS THAT REMINDER IN YOUR DIARY? HOW DID YOUR DISCUSSION WITH YOUR FRIENDS AND FAMILY GO – DO YOU FEEL MORE BREAST AWARE THAN YOU WERE?

....

....

So Loved

HOW HAVE YOU GONE IMPLEMENTING MORE SELF-CARE INTO YOUR DAY-TO-DAY? HOW WILL YOU CONTINUE TO MAKE THIS A PRIORITY GOING FORWARD?

....

....

So Cherished

HOW DO YOU FEEL IN YOUR RELATIONSHIPS? HOW DO YOU FEEL ABOUT THE FUTURE AND WHO YOU SHARE YOUR LIFE WITH?

....

....

So Mindful

HAVE YOU BEEN CHECKING IN WITH YOURSELF MORE REGULARLY? WHERE ANY CONCERNS HAVE BEEN ACKNOWLEDGED, HAVE YOU TAKEN STEPS TO SEEK SUPPORT? IF ANYTHING, WHAT'S HOLDING YOU BACK?

....

....

So Courageous

WHAT LIGHTS YOU UP AND FIRES YOUR PASSION? HOW DO YOU WANT TO GIVE BACK?

....

....

So Savvy

DO YOU HAVE A BETTER UNDERSTANDING OF YOUR FINANCES? DO YOU HAVE A PLAN FOR THE FUTURE - WHAT DOES IT LOOK LIKE? WHAT'S THAT ONE SPECIAL FINANCIAL GOAL THAT YOU'RE WORKING TOWARDS?

....

....

So Confident

WHAT DOES COURAGE AND SELF-UNDERSTANDING LOOK LIKE TO YOU NOW? WHAT ELSE CAN YOU WORK ON, AND WHAT AREAS OF YOUR LIFE DO YOU WANT TO BUILD YOUR CONFIDENCE?

....

....

So Healthy

HAVE YOU FOUND SOME WAYS TO INCORPORATE HEALTHY PRACTICES INTO YOUR LIFE? WHAT ARE YOUR HEALTH AND FITNESS GOALS FOR THE NEXT 3 MONTHS?

....

....

So Powerful

HAVE YOU MADE THOSE APPOINTMENTS TO GET YOUR CHECKS? WHAT ELSE DO YOU NEED TO CONSIDER IN LOVING YOUR BEAUTIFUL SELF?

....

....

Thank you

Thank you so much for your support of this first-of So Brave publication. We hope you had as much fun reading the stories and doing the exercises as we did in collating it! If any of the exercises have brought up concerns for you, please be sure to talk with friends and family and most importantly, to seek help. We're excited to continue the discussion with you over in our exclusive facebook group and to talk with more experts on each of these topics – thank you for joining us on this transformational journey to help you to become *Me: Without Reservation*.

Nothing is impossible. The word itself says, 'I'm possible!

AUDREY HEPBURN

keep in touch

ABOUT SO BRAVE

So Brave, as the only breast cancer charity in Australia specifically advocating for and representing young women, has worked with hundreds of young women over the past 5 years. So Brave Founder and Managing Director Rachelle Panitz's breast cancer diagnosis at 32 inspired her to advocate for the nearly 1000 Australian young women diagnosed with breast cancer annually. So Brave's mission is to empower young women to be their best health advocates, collaborating on and funding research into breast cancer and education for young women.

SOBRAVE.COM.AU /SOBRAVEPROJECT

ABOUT BRAVE|YOU

Brave|You is So Brave's Young Women's Advisory Committee is a collective of young women aged 15-25.

Brave|You is a committee that is with, by and for young women; valuing empowerment, advocacy and authenticity, with the dual aims to promote breast awareness in young women and self-advocacy skills across a wide range of health and life issues for young women. Brave|You members are passionate about self-advocacy and want to work with, by and for their peers to change health outcomes and conversations for young women in Australia.

Under the So Brave banner, Brave|You allows young women to take leadership and community advocacy roles, in the breast awareness space but also on a wide range of health topics in addition to breast health and awareness.

Focusing on engaging with young women aged 15-25, the advisory committee aims to establish smaller geographic and demographic committees at universities and high schools across Australia.

Young women interested in getting involved should contact the committee at
SOBRAVE.COM.AU/BRAVEYOU /WITHBYFOR

www.ingramcontent.com/pod-product-compliance
Lightning Source LLC
Chambersburg PA
CBHW041459010526
44107CB00044B/1505